High-Interest/Low-Readability Nonfiction

Amazing Kids

by Kathryn Wheeler

Carson-Dellosa Publishing Company, Inc.
Greensboro, North Carolina

Credits

Editor:
Ashley Anderson

Layout Design:
Van Harris

Inside Illustrations:
Donald O'Connor

Cover Design:
Annette Hollister-Papp
Peggy Jackson

Cover Illustration:
Tara Tavonatti

ISBN 1-59441-330-4

Table of Contents

Introduction

Struggling readers in the upper-elementary and middle grades face a difficult challenge. While many of their peers are reading fluently, they are still working to acquire vocabulary and comprehension skills. They face a labyrinth of standardized tests, which can be a nightmare for struggling readers. And, they face another major difficulty—the challenge of remaining engaged and interested while working to improve reading skills.

High-Interest/Low-Readability Nonfiction: Amazing Kids can help! All of the articles in this book are written at a fourth-grade reading level with an interest level from grade 4 to adult.

Throughout the book, the stories use repeated vocabulary to help students acquire and practice new words. The stories are crafted to grab students' attention while honing specific reading skills, such as uncovering author's purpose; defining vocabulary; making predictions; and identifying details, synonyms, antonyms, and figures of speech. Most of the comprehension questions parallel standardized-test formats so that students can become familiar with the structure without the pressure of a testing situation. And, the articles even utilize the familiar "Next Page" arrows and "Stop" signs seen in most standardized tests. The questions also include short-answer formats for writing practice.

Best of all, this book will build confidence in students as they learn that reading is fun, enjoyable, and fascinating!

Note: Stories that include measurements, such as a height or weight, also feature a convenient conversion box with measurements rounded to the nearest hundredth. Students will find this useful as they become familiar with converting standard and metric measurements. If students are not currently studying measurement conversion, simply instruct them to ignore the box. Or, cover it when making copies of a story.

Olympic Spirit

It would have been very easy for **Wilma Rudolph** to give up. She was a small and sickly child. She only weighed 4.5 pounds when she was born. In the first years of her life, Wilma's mother helped her when she had the measles, the mumps, chicken pox, and scarlet fever because the family could not afford a doctor. Then, things became even more serious. Wilma got *pneumonia*, an illness that causes the lungs to fill with fluid. After beating pneumonia, Wilma's parents saw that one of her legs was weak.

The Rudolph family was very poor. This time, they had to pay for a doctor. The news was not good. Wilma had *polio*. Polio is an illness that can cripple legs or arms. Today, there are shots that protect people from polio. But, Wilma was born in 1940 before the shots were created.

The doctor told Wilma's parents that she would never walk. Wilma had a different idea. The doctor put braces on her legs. Wilma said that she was always trying to take them off. Wilma's brothers and sisters watched her to make sure she kept the braces on. They helped rub her legs to make them better. Wilma also went to the hospital once a week. It was very hard work to make her legs strong. But, Wilma was brave. When she was 11 years old, Wilma took off her braces forever.

What did Wilma want to do after spending her whole life barely able to walk? She wanted to play sports! She started by playing basketball. Even after she joined a team, three years passed before her coach would let her play. Wilma did not give up. When her coach finally let her play, she set a state record. That was only the beginning! Wilma Rudolph went on to become a great track star. She won three gold medals in the 1960 Olympics. She was the first woman to do that. It was a long trip from her sickness-filled childhood to the Olympics. Wilma Rudolph made it because of her brave childhood.

Conversion

4.5 pounds = 2.04 kilograms

Olympic Spirit

Answer the questions below.

1. Wilma Rudolph became—
    a. a famous track star.
    b. a famous baseball player.
    c. the first woman to fly.
    d. a famous politician.

2. Read the following sentence from the story and answer the question.

    The doctor put braces on her legs.

    Which of the following definitions of *braces* is used in this sentence?

    a. clasps that hold things together
    b. suspenders
    c. metal supports for the body
    d. plant firmly

3. Circle three adjectives that tell about Wilma Rudolph as a child.

    fast   poor   sickly

    healthy   angry   brave

4. Finish these sentences about Wilma Rudolph at the Olympics.

    Wilma Rudolph was the first

    _____ to win

    three gold medals at the Olympics.

    She won her medals in the year

    _____ .

5. What is *track*?
    a. sporting events that feature passing a ball
    b. a game like hockey
    c. sporting events that feature running
    d. none of the above

6. Read the following sentences from the story and answer the question.

    The news was not good. Wilma had *polio*.

    What is *polio*?
    a. It is an illness that causes blindness.
    b. It is an illness that causes the lungs to fill with fluid.
    c. It is an illness that can cripple arms and legs.
    d. It is an illness that causes scarlet fever.

To the Stars

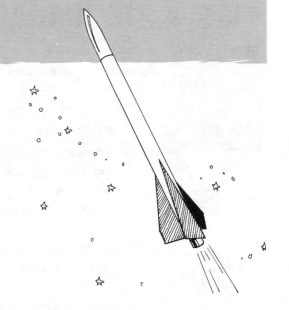

In Coalwood, West Virginia, many boys became miners when they grew up. That's what **Homer Hickam** could have done, too. The mine owners owned the entire town of Coalwood. Mining was hard work. Sometimes, there was great danger. But, it was all that the town knew how to do. Homer's own father wanted him to work for the mine. That was before the rockets.

In 1957, Homer was 14 years old. Russian scientists had put the first satellite, called *Sputnik*, into space. Homer watched it streak through the sky while standing with the other people of his town. That's when Homer decided to build his own rocket. He and five friends built one together. It blew up the fence outside of Homer's house!

Instead of giving up, Homer started to read. His teacher, Miss Riley, gave him a book. In order to understand it, Homer learned some hard math. He did it. Homer and his friends helped each other. They built 11 more rockets. All of them failed. People in town started calling them "The Rocket Boys."

The Rocket Boys learned everything they could about math and science. They changed the way that they built the rockets. Then, they put everything that they learned into a science fair project. They won a national gold medal for their work.

By 1960, The Rocket Boys had built 31 rockets. The last one was over five feet tall. Almost everyone in the town came to watch the rocket go into the air. It was the last rocket that Homer built in Coalwood. But, the rockets had changed his life. He ended up working for the United States government at NASA instead of in the coal mine. His dreams took him to the stars.

Conversion

5 feet = 1.52 meters

Next Page

Name_____ Date_____

To the Stars

Answer the questions below.

1. What did Homer Hickam decide to do when he was 14?

    a. He wanted to build a satellite.
    b. He decided to blow up a fence.
    c. He wanted to fly in *Sputnik*.
    d. none of the above

2. Read the following sentence from the story and answer the question.

    Homer watched it streak through the sky while standing with the other people of his town.

    What is another word for *streak*?

    a. stream
    b. stretch
    c. race
    d. wander

3. In order to build his rockets, Homer had to do all of the following EXCEPT—

    a. learn how to fly.
    b. learn more science.
    c. learn difficult math.
    d. get help from his friends.

4. What was *Sputnik*? Write your answer in complete sentences.

    _____

    _____

    _____

    _____

5. Homer and his friends won a gold medal at—

    a. NASA.
    b. a local science fair.
    c. Coalwood.
    d. a national science fair.

6. What is NASA?

    a. It is the part of the government that builds rockets and satellites.
    b. It is a company that owns and sails large ships.
    c. It is the part of the government that trains astronauts.
    d. a. and c.

7. How did the rockets change Homer's life? Write your answer in complete sentences.

    _____

    _____

    _____

    _____

    _____

    _____

    _____

Behind the Bookcase

Anne Frank was only four years old when the nightmare started for her family. Her father decided that he had to move his family from Germany to Holland. They fled because they were Jews. The Nazis were taking power. Otto Frank knew that the Jews in Germany were in danger.

Anne liked her new life in Holland. She made new friends. She went to school. But then, World War II started. The Nazis took over Holland, and the nightmare started again. Otto Frank had to find a safe place to hide his family. He owned a building with offices and workrooms. He built a secret place behind a bookcase in one of the offices. The bookcase moved away from the wall. It was the door to the hiding place. The Frank family and another family moved there in 1942. Anne had just had a birthday. She took her present with her. It was a blank diary. While she was living in the hiding place, she wrote in her diary every day.

Two long years passed. The families lived in their secret place. They could not walk or move during the day. The workers below might hear them. They could only talk, cook, and walk at night. They never went outside. They were very careful. But, the Nazis still found them. They were arrested in 1944. They were taken to a prison camp. Only Otto Frank lived to see the end of the war.

Something else survived, too. Anne's diary was still behind the bookcase in the secret rooms. It told the story of their life in hiding. Even though she was only 13 years old when she started it, Anne's diary showed that she was a fine writer. All of the things she hoped for and feared were written down. Her father thought other people should read Anne's diary. The book was printed and released in 1949. This moving story about the lives of two Jewish families during World War II is still read today. In it, Anne's amazing spirit is still alive.

Next Page →

Behind the Bookcase

Answer the questions below.

1. Read the following sentence from the story and answer the question.

   This moving story about the lives of two Jewish families during World War II is still read today.

   Which of the following definitions of the word *moving* is used in the sentence?

   a. traveling from one place to another
   b. carrying furniture to a new place
   c. a kind of ticket for a car accident
   d. deeply touching

2. Why did Anne and her family have to go into hiding? Write your answer in a complete sentence.

   _____

   _____

3. Which of these is NOT a feature of the Frank family's hiding place?

   a. had a door so that they could go outside at night
   b. had a doorway hidden behind a bookcase
   c. housed two families
   d. was in an office building

4.–8. Write T for true and F for false.

4. _____ Anne was two years old when her family left Germany.

5. _____ The Nazis took over Holland after World War II started.

6. _____ Anne wrote about their hiding place on a computer.

7. _____ Two families hid in the secret rooms in the office building.

8. _____ Otto Frank had Anne's diary published after the war ended.

9. Choose the number that BEST completes this sentence:

   Anne was _____ years old when her family was arrested.

   a. 4
   b. 12
   c. 13
   d. 15

10. During the day, the people in the

    hiding place could not _____

    _____

    because _____

    _____

    _____ .

Musical Stories

Leon Buche was born in Germany in 1988. One day when he was four years old, he sat down at the piano. He started to play songs that he made up himself. He is still making up music. This is called *composing*. Today, his music is played in Germany and across Europe.

Leon goes to a special school for musicians. At the school, he studies all kinds of things about music. Many students at the school learn how to play instruments. Leon spends much of his time writing music. He says that making music is easy for him. He writes many works for the piano. He gets his ideas when he is outside. Sometimes he rides horses, and sometimes he watches the sun set. Then, he writes his music.

Leon started to write his first full-length piece of music when he was 12 years old. This kind of work is called a *symphony*. The music is based on a popular book called *Harry Potter and the Sorcerer's Stone*.[1] Each character has a melody of his or her own. Each part of the story is told in music. The entire piece is 45 minutes long.

After that, Leon started a new work. This piece tells the story of the June 17 Uprising. After World War II, Germany was split into two parts. Part of the country was given to the Soviet Union. In 1953, people rose up against this. They marched in the streets. They said that they wanted to be free. But, it took almost 40 years for Germany to become one country again.

Leon's second symphony was played in Berlin in 2004. What will he do next? Leon has said that he might like to write music for movies. For now, he is still writing music for important concerts. He also writes music for the band at his school!

[1] *Harry Potter and the Sorcerer's Stone* by J. K. Rowling (Scholastic Paperbacks, 1999).

Musical Stories

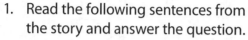

Answer the questions below.

1. Read the following sentences from the story and answer the question.

   He started to play songs that he made up himself. He is still making up music.

   What is another word for *making up music*?

   a. symphony
   b. compiling
   c. composing
   d. collecting

2. Which of the following things did Leon Buche use to write a work of music?

   a. a German fairy tale
   b. a Harry Potter book
   c. an important date in history
   d. b. and c.

3. Leon Buche was _____ years old when he started to play the piano.

4. A _____ is a full-length piece of music.

5. Leon learns about music at a special _____ .

6. After World War II, Germany was _____ .

7. When Leon grows up, he might like to—

   a. give piano lessons.
   b. write music for movies.
   c. teach music at his school.
   d. write Harry Potter stories.

8. Choose the BEST phrase to complete the following sentence:

   Leon Buche wrote _____ when he was 12 years old.

   a. his first symphony
   b. his piece about Harry Potter
   c. his piece about the June 17 Uprising
   d. a. and b.

9. If you wrote a piece of music about a story, what story would you choose? Why? Write your answer in complete sentences.

   _____

   _____

   _____

   _____

   _____

STOP

A Mind for Math

Can you multiply numbers in your head? How about 7,686,369,774,870 times 2,465,099,745,799? That's just one problem that **Shakuntala Devi** multiplied in her head. She didn't even have a piece of paper to help her! And, she finished the problem in only 28 seconds.

This famous math wizard from India had very little schooling. She came from a poor family. But, she could solve hard math problems by the time she was three years old. Her father loved to do card tricks. Shakuntala could always tell what card he would pull from the deck. How did she do it? By learning the order of the cards and remembering them.

Shakuntala was so good at numbers that she went on stage to show her skills. By the time she was eight years old, she had traveled all over India. She had also gone to Europe. She could do all kinds of math problems. She was also good at *calendar problems*. If someone said a date in history, Shakuntala could instantly figure out the day of the week for that date.

Shakuntala was born in 1939. When she was young, one computer was so big that it filled a whole room. Shakuntala could do math problems much faster than those early machines. Once, she had to find the square root of a number that was 201 digits long. She found the answer. The computer that was checking her work took 10 seconds longer than Shakuntala did.

In fact, Shakuntala thinks that people use computers too much. She also thinks that students should not use calculators. She thinks that the brain needs exercise, just like other parts of the body. If Shakuntala had her way, students would not use computers or calculators until they went to college. Until then, their brains would be able to get a real workout!

Name _____ Date _____

A Mind for Math

Answer the questions below.

1. What is a *calendar problem*? Write your answer in a complete sentence.

   _____

   _____

   _____

   _____

2. Which of the following is NOT in the story?

   a. when Shakuntala Devi was born
   b. where Shakuntala Devi is today
   c. what kinds of math problems Shakuntala Devi can do
   d. how old Shakuntala Devi was when she started doing math problems

3.–7. Write T for true and F for false.

3. _____ Shakuntala needs to use a calculator for big numbers.

4. _____ Shakuntala could do math faster than early computers.

5. _____ Shakuntala Devi is from India.

6. _____ Shakuntala came from a rich family.

7. _____ Shakuntala memorized the cards in her father's card tricks.

8. Read the following sentence from the story and answer the question.

   Once, she had to find the square root of a number that was 201 digits long.

   What is the definition of *root* as it is used in this sentence?

   a. part of a plant
   b. mathematical base
   c. part of a tooth
   d. simplest part of a word

9. By the time Shakuntala was _____ years old, she had traveled all over India.

   a. three
   b. five
   c. seven
   d. eight

10. Why does Shakuntala think students should not have computers or calculators until they are in college? Write your answer in a complete sentence.

    _____

    _____

    _____

    _____

STOP

The Boy King

Edward VI was only nine years old when he became the king of England in 1547. On the day he was crowned, Edward could already speak Latin, French, and English. He understood how battles were fought. He knew the names of all of the families at his court.

Edward was the son of King Henry VIII. He had two sisters, Mary and Elizabeth. Each of them became queen after he died. All three of these children were very smart. But, many people think that Edward was a genius.

Because he was a prince, Edward started to study when he was young. He learned how to read when he was very small. By the time he was seven years old, he could read stories in Latin. By the time he was 11 years old, Edward could speak six languages: French, Latin, Greek, Spanish, Italian, and English. His teachers were amazed by how fast he learned.

Edward had to learn many things other than languages. He had to know how to plan wars. So, Edward learned geography. Before his sixth birthday, he knew the names of all of the towns and rivers on the coast of Europe. He read about famous battles. He learned how to fight with a sword.

By the time he became king, Edward also had learned other things that he needed to know to rule a country. He remembered the family histories of all of the people at court. He understood how England's money system worked. He knew how to speak with *diplomats*, or people sent to his court by other kings. Very few people understood how to do these things as well as Edward did them.

Many people think that Edward would have been one of the greatest kings to ever rule England. Sadly, he died when he was only 15 years old.

Next Page

Name _____ Date _____

The Boy King

Answer the questions below.

1. Read the following sentence from the story and answer the question.

   But, many people think that Edward was a genius.

   What is a *genius*?

   a. a person who writes well
   b. a person with amazing skills and knowledge
   c. a person who becomes a king
   d. a person who can play music

2. Edward VI was the son of—

   a. Queen Mary I of England.
   b. Queen Elizabeth I of England.
   c. King Henry VI of England.
   d. none of the above

3. How many languages could Edward speak?

   a. three
   b. five
   c. six
   d. nine

4. Why did Edward have to learn geography?

   a. so that he could find places to travel
   b. so that he could learn to sail
   c. so that he could plan battles and wars
   d. so that he could meet other kings

5. A *diplomat* is—

   a. someone who is sent to the court by another king or queen.
   b. someone who teaches languages.
   c. someone who writes books.
   d. someone who can fight with a sword.

6. Which of the following sentences BEST states the main idea of this story?

   a. King Edward VI was very talented and smart, but he died when he was only 10 years old.
   b. Edward VI might have been one of the greatest kings of all time, but he died young.
   c. Edward VI was only nine years old when he became a king.
   d. Other people thought that Edward VI was smarter than his sisters.

7. I think one of the hardest things that Edward VI had to learn was

   _____

   because _____

   _____

   _____ .

A Novel Approach

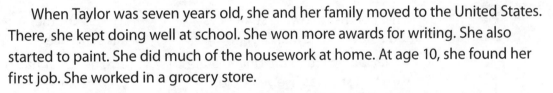

Taylor Caldwell was born in 1900. Her family lived in England. Her parents were very strict. Taylor had many chores to do. After her baby brother was born, Taylor also helped to take care of him. When Taylor was only five years old, she won a national gold medal. It was for an essay she had written at school. By the time she was six years old, Taylor was learning to read in French and Latin.

When Taylor was seven years old, she and her family moved to the United States. There, she kept doing well at school. She won more awards for writing. She also started to paint. She did much of the housework at home. At age 10, she found her first job. She worked in a grocery store.

By the time Taylor was 15, she had a full-time job. She worked as a secretary. After her 10-hour work days, she went to high school at night. On the weekends, she spent her time cleaning her family's house, cooking, and doing her homework. She almost never had a free minute.

Taylor was very busy. But, she found the time to write stories. She started writing fiction when she was eight years old. By the time she was 12, she had written an entire novel. It was called *The Romance of Atlantis*. The book was about a lost kingdom and its ruler. The story told about a war between Atlantis and another country. The novel was published much later in Taylor's life. Nobody could believe it had been written by a 12-year-old!

Taylor went on to become a very famous writer. She wrote 30 novels. Many of them were best-sellers. Late in her life, she said that all of the hard work during her childhood got her ready for a lifetime of writing books.

A Novel Approach

Answer the questions below.

1. Read the following sentence from the story and answer the question.

   When Taylor was only five years old, she won a national gold medal.

   Why did Taylor win the medal?

   a. It was for a book that she wrote.
   b. It was for a poem that she wrote.
   c. It was for an essay that she wrote.
   d. It was for a play that she wrote.

2. Which of the following sentences about Taylor Caldwell is true?

   a. Taylor moved to the United States when she was five years old.
   b. Taylor started writing fiction when she was eight years old.
   c. Taylor had to go to work when she was nine years old.
   d. Taylor wanted to write stories, but her parents wouldn't let her.

3. When Taylor started working full time, how did she finish school?

   a. She went to school in the evenings.
   b. She went to school on the weekends.
   c. She was home-schooled.
   d. b. and c.

4. How old was Taylor when she wrote her first book?

   _____

5. What was the name of Taylor's first novel?

   a. *The Lost Kingdom*
   b. *My Love of Atlantis*
   c. *The Romance of Atlantis*
   d. *The Lost Romance*

6. Read the following sentence from the story and answer the question.

   She almost never had a free minute.

   What is another way of writing this sentence?

   a. She never had minutes to give away.
   b. She never had time to spare.
   c. She was always late for everything.
   d. She was paid for all of the housework she did.

7. If you wrote a novel, what would it be about? Write your answer in a complete sentence.

   _____

   _____

   _____

   _____

Mozart's Young Life

Some people take a long time to learn new skills. Other people seem to be born with talent. That was true of **Wolfgang Amadeus Mozart**. When he was an adult, he was one of the most famous composers of all time. But, he was also brilliant as a small child.

When he was three years old, Mozart started to play songs on the piano. When he was five, he started to write his own music. His father was a musician, too. He took the young Mozart on tours to the royal courts of kings and queens. Mozart played all over Europe. He could play perfectly, even when he was blindfolded and couldn't see the keys. His father held him over the piano, and the upside-down boy could still play! He amazed the people who came to hear him.

Mozart started to publish his music when he was only seven years old. By the time he was eight, he had taught himself how to play the organ and the violin. He also wrote a *symphony*, a full-length piece of music. He was only 13 years old when he wrote his first *opera*. An opera is a work that is acted out like a play, with singing parts instead of speaking parts.

Because he traveled so much, Mozart was hardly ever at home. He was not really happy. Very few people were as smart as he was. But, in some ways, Mozart was not smart. He spent too much money. When he left his father and went to live on his own, he found it hard to make enough money. Mozart died when he was only 35 years old. His works are still played and loved all over the world today.

Name_____ Date_____

Mozart's Young Life

Answer the questions below.

1.–5. Match each word to its antonym.

1. _____amazing   a. sad

2. _____happy   b. upright

3. _____brilliant   c. common

4. _____upside-down   d. ordinary

5. _____royal   e. dull

6. Read the following sentence from the story and answer the question.

   He could play perfectly, even when he was blindfolded so that he couldn't see the keys.

   Which of the following is a synonym for *perfectly*?
   a. mistakenly
   b. badly
   c. faultlessly
   d. charmingly

7. Circle the correct word or phrase in parentheses to complete each of the following sentences.

   a. People (**do** , **do not**) play Mozart's music today.

   b. Mozart (**was** , **was not**) good at handling money.

   c. Mozart died when he was (**23** , **35** , **48**) years old.

8. What is an *opera*?
   a. a full-length piece of music
   b. a play with parts that are played silently
   c. a kind of game played at court
   d. a play with parts that are sung

9. Finish the following sentences.
   a. Mozart could play the piano, organ, and _____.

   b. Mozart was _____ years old when his music was first published.

   c. Mozart traveled across Europe with his _____.

10. How do you think Mozart could have had a happier life? Write your answer in a complete sentence.

   _____

   _____

   _____

   _____

The Gravity of Childhood

Sir Isaac Newton was the first person to be able to explain gravity. He was a very important scientist and thinker. But, the start of his life was hard. He overcame many troubles to become successful later in his life.

Isaac was born on Christmas Day in 1642. His father had just died. When Isaac was three years old, his mother married again. Her new husband did not want Isaac. So, the little boy was raised by his grandmother.

When Isaac started school, he was far behind the other boys in his class. He was second from the last in his grade! Things did not look good for Isaac Newton. But, he was a good learner. He spent much of his time outside. He flew kites and watched how the wind moved them. He watched the clouds and the stars. He carved models and played with them. Once, he made a little windmill. It was powered by a mouse running on a treadmill. He was always busy. He was always thinking.

All of his work paid off. By the time Isaac left school, he was first in his class. All of the time he spent watching the world paid off, too. One day, Isaac was sitting at home and looking out a window. He saw an apple fall from a tree. Suddenly, he wondered why apples always fall to the ground. Why don't they fall up to the sky? Why don't they fall sideways? Each apple always falls toward the center of the earth. That was when Isaac first started thinking about *gravity*, the force that pulls things toward the earth. It was only one of his important ideas. He also worked math problems. He was the first person who thought about gravity and the orbit of the moon. He also wrote about color and light. Isaac Newton had many of his famous ideas during his lonely but thoughtful childhood. Today, students still study his ideas in science classes around the world.

Next Page

The Gravity of Childhood

Answer the questions below.

1. _____ is the force that pulls things toward the earth.

2. Sir Isaac Newton was born on

   _____

   in the year _____ .

3. Even though he was not a good student at first, Isaac Newton was a good _____ .

4. In order to study the wind, Isaac flew

   _____ .

5. Isaac Newton lived with his

   _____ after he

   was three years old.

6.–9. Write T for true and F for false.

6. _____ One of Isaac Newton's ideas was about how gravity affects the moon's orbit.

7. _____ Isaac first thought about gravity when he saw a squirrel jump out of a tree.

8. _____ Isaac built a little model of an airplane.

9. _____ Another idea that Isaac explored was about color and light.

10. Read the following sentence from the story and answer the question.

    All of his work paid off.

    Which phrase could replace *paid off* in the sentence?
    a. made him poor
    b. was rewarding
    c. made him tired
    d. paid his bills

11. In your opinion, what was Isaac Newton's most important idea? Why do you think so? Write your answer in complete sentences.

    _____

    _____

    _____

    _____

    _____

STOP

The Violin as a Voice

Sarah Chang says that the violin is the closest music to the human voice. She has been hearing that voice most of her life. Sarah was only three years old when she begged her parents for a violin. She learned how to play it right away. Her parents, both musicians, helped her. But, even they were amazed when she was accepted into a famous music school called Juilliard when she was only five years old!

Sarah's father was her first teacher. He also plays violin. Her mother is a *composer*, or someone who writes music. She helped Sarah learn about reading and understanding music. Sarah's gift for playing, though, seems to have been with her all of her life.

Sarah's entire life has been wrapped up in her musical talent. She started to play with orchestras when she was eight years old. By the time she was nine, she had recorded some of her music on CDs. People love to hear her play. A famous musician named Yehudi Menuhin said that Sarah was the most perfect violinist he had ever heard.

Sarah also speaks three languages. She speaks Korean because her parents are from Korea. She also speaks German and English. Sarah travels often to play with different orchestras. She says that her entire life is planned. If you ask her where she will be two years from now, she knows what hotel she will be staying in and what she will be practicing on her violin. Sometimes, she doesn't like that. She wishes that she had more free time. But, she says if she doesn't touch a violin for three or four days, her fingers start to miss playing. She also says she loves to be on the stage playing music for other people. For her, that's the most important thing in life.

Next Page

The Violin as a Voice

Answer the questions below.

1. Which of the following is an opinion?

   a. Sarah Chang started to play violin when she was three years old.
   b. Sarah Chang first learned violin from her father.
   c. Sarah Chang is the most perfect violinist in the world.
   d. Sarah Chang went to a special music school.

2. Which of the following sentences is NOT true?

   a. Yehudi Menuhin is a famous musician.
   b. Sarah Chang rarely travels to play her music.
   c. Sarah does not like to stop playing violin for more than a few days.
   d. By the time Sarah was nine years old, she had recorded her first CD.

3. Read the following sentence from the story and answer the question.

   She wishes that she had more free time.

   What is another phrase that the author could have used in place of *more free time*?

   a. more leisure time
   b. more paid time
   c. more scheduled time
   d. more practice time

4. How much time passed between when Sarah got her first violin and when she started school at Juilliard?

   a. 6 months
   b. 1 year
   c. 12 months
   d. 2 years

5. Which of the following is NOT mentioned in the story?

   a. Sarah's birth date
   b. Sarah's parents and their jobs
   c. Sarah's age when she started playing her violin with orchestras
   d. the languages that Sarah speaks

6. Do you think you would like to have a life like Sarah's? Why or why not? Write your answer in complete sentences.

   _____

   _____

   _____

   _____

   _____

   _____

The Peacemaker

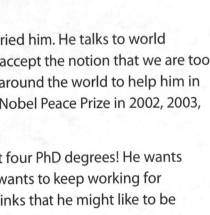

Gregory Smith likes to read. Some of his favorite books are by Jules Verne. He started reading Verne's books when he was in kindergarten. His classmates were still learning the alphabet. Gregory says it was then that he knew he was different from other children.

Gregory's parents decided that he needed to go to a school where he could learn as fast as he wanted. They moved to Florida. Gregory started high school there when he was seven years old. He finished high school when he was 10. It took him three years to finish college. Then, he started graduate school to work on his *PhD*, a doctor's degree, in math.

Is that all Gregory has done? If so, he would still be an amazing kid! But, that is only part of Gregory's story. He also works for children around the world. He started this work when he was seven years old. He starts programs to help children. He meets with world leaders. He tells them that children are important. Gregory feels that peace is linked to the well-being of children.

The fact that Gregory is so young has never worried him. He talks to world leaders without fear. Gregory says, "We must never accept the notion that we are too young for our voices to be heard." He asks children around the world to help him in his work for peace. Gregory was nominated for the Nobel Peace Prize in 2002, 2003, 2004, and 2005.

What will Gregory do next? First, he plans to get four PhD degrees! He wants to finish them all by the time he is 27 years old. He wants to keep working for the world's children and for world peace. He also thinks that he might like to be President of the United States someday.

Next Page

The Peacemaker

Answer the questions below.

1. Read the following sentence from the story and answer the question.

   Gregory says, "We must never accept the notion that we are too young for our voices to be heard."

   What is a word that could replace *notion* in this sentence?

   a. demand
   b. attempt
   c. idea
   d. sense

2. What is a *graduate school*?

   a. a school that students can go to before college
   b. a school that students can go to after they finish college
   c. a school that students can go to between middle school and high school
   d. none of the above

3. Based on the story, what can you infer about the difference between Gregory Smith and other students in his kindergarten class?

   a. His classmates were learning at a normal pace, and he was not.
   b. He could read when he started kindergarten.
   c. The class was not challenging for him.
   d. all of the above

4. The story describes all of the following facts about Gregory Smith EXCEPT—

   a. his age when he started college.
   b. his work for children.
   c. his plan to get PhD degrees.
   d. his place of birth.

5.–8. Write T for true and F for false.

5. _____ Gregory Smith finished high school when he was 10.

6. _____ Gregory talks to world leaders about helping children.

7. _____ Gregory wants four PhD degrees; the first one is in math.

8. _____ Gregory would like to be the president of a college someday.

9. What is one thing you would say if you could meet with a world leader? Write your answer in a complete sentence.

   _____

   _____

   _____

Culture Clash

A man thinks he is about to be put to death. Other men are standing all around him, holding clubs. Suddenly, a 12-year-old girl runs to him. She throws her arms around the man's head. She pulls the man to his feet. His life is saved!

This is the story that John Smith, an English settler in the New World, told about the first time he saw **Pocahontas**. Smith met a powerful Native American chief named Powhatan. The chief asked Smith to feast with him. But then, the mood of the event turned dark. Smith was held down. He was stretched over some large, flat rocks. Tribe members held clubs, as if they planned to hurt him. Did Powhatan's young daughter, Pocahontas, really save John Smith's life?

Some writers say no. They say that what took place was really a *ceremony*, a kind of play that the tribe performed. It showed that a stranger was now a friend. Maybe Pocahontas was just playing a part in the event. Today, some members of the tribe say that Pocahontas did not even like John Smith. Other people say she thought of him as a father. There are many different stories about the two of them.

We do know that Pocahontas played a big part in the real-life link between her tribe and the settlers of Jamestown. She helped bring peace between them. She took messages from her father to the settlers. She asked her father to give the settlers food. Later, Pocahontas even married a settler. His name was John Rolfe. The wedding also helped to bring peace between the two groups.

John Rolfe took his new wife to England for a visit. Pocahontas wanted to go back home, but it was not meant to be. In 1617, she became ill and died just before she and John were scheduled to sail home.

Next Page ➜

Culture Clash

Answer the questions below.

1. Read the following sentence from the story and answer the question.

   Today, some members of the tribe say that Pocahontas did not even like John Smith.

   Why do you think that the author included this fact?

   a. It's important to learn different ideas about this historical event.
   b. It's important to know that some people did not like John Smith.
   c. The author wanted to confuse the reader.
   d. none of the above

2. Who was Pocahontas?

   a. the daughter of a chief named Powhatan
   b. a person who helped the settlers in Jamestown
   c. a Native American woman who married a man from England
   d. all of the above

3. Which of the following sentences does NOT contain an opinion?

   a. Maybe Pocahontas was just playing a part in a play when she saved John Smith.
   b. It really seemed that the tribe wanted to kill John Smith.
   c. Pocahontas married an Englishman.
   d. Pocahontas is one of the most interesting people in history.

4. Which of the following sentences BEST summarizes the main idea of the story?

   a. Although we do not know who Pocahontas was, we still talk about her today.
   b. We do not know all of the facts about Pocahontas, but we do know that she helped the settlers in Jamestown.
   c. We do not know if Pocahontas really liked John Smith or not.
   d. We do not know anything about the life or death of Pocahontas.

5. When Pocahontas met John Smith, she was _____ years old.

6. Pocahontas married an Englishman named John _____ .

7. What are three ways that Pocahontas helped the settlers of Jamestown?

   a. _____

   b. _____

   c. _____

A Life in Poetry

Mattie Stepanek was born with a burden and a gift. The burden was an illness called *muscular dystrophy* (MD). This is a serious illness that makes the muscles weak. It makes it hard to breathe. Like all children who have this disease, Mattie knew that he would die from it. But, he also had a gift: his ability to love life anyway.

Instead of feeling sorry for himself, Mattie started to write poetry and give speeches. He first created poems when he was only three years old. He spoke his poems into a tape recorder because he was too little to write them down. Later, he started to write essays and stories, too, but his poetry is best known. He called his poems "heartsongs." The books of these poems became best-sellers.

Mattie also worked to help other children who had MD. Because he had a rare kind of MD, the doctors learned a lot from studying him. He spoke at events for MD and helped raise money for research. As he became more ill, this became harder. Mattie needed to be in a wheelchair. He needed air to help him breathe. But, he still worked hard to help people. "People tell me I inspire them," Mattie said once. "And that inspires me. It's a beautiful circle."

Mattie died in June 2004, at the age of 13. But, his books and his life still help people. Mattie's brave view of life helped him to make a difference. Mattie said that a hero never gives up. If that is true, then Mattie Stepanek was a hero who had an amazing life.

A Life in Poetry

Answer the questions below.

1. What is *muscular dystrophy*?
   a. an illness that attacks the muscles
   b. an illness that makes it hard to breathe
   c. a. and b.
   d. none of the above

2. Read the following sentence from the story and answer the question.

   "People tell me I inspire them," Mattie said once.

   What does *inspire* mean?

   a. to move someone to new thoughts or actions
   b. to learn something important
   c. to breathe easily
   d. to find a way that was lost

3. What did Mattie call his poems?
   a. heartbeats
   b. heart-thoughts
   c. heartsongs
   d. heartsinging

4. List three words or phrases from the story that describe Mattie Stepanek.

   a. _____

   b. _____

   c. _____

5. Why do you think it would have been easy for Mattie to have given up on life? Write your answer in a complete sentence.

   _____

   _____

   _____

   _____

6. According to the author, what gift did Mattie have?
   a. the ability to love life
   b. the ability to paint pictures
   c. the ability to play sports
   d. the ability to learn different languages

7. What was one way that Mattie helped other people? Write your answer in a complete sentence.

   _____

   _____

   _____

   _____

STOP

Movie History

Stephen Spielberg loved to play jokes on his sisters when he was young. But, there was one thing that he was serious about: movies. Today, this talented man has made some of the most famous films of all time. His work started when he was a kid.

When he was 12 years old, Stephen found an old movie camera in his garage. Stephen was in the Boy Scouts. He had been asked to take photos for a project. Instead, he made a movie. His first movie, *The Last Train Wreck*, was only three minutes long. Stephen wanted to make a longer and better movie, but he needed money. He started a tree-selling business. He used the money he earned to buy film for his camera and supplies. The movie he made next, *The Last Gun*, was a western.

Stephen was hooked. He did not waste any time before he started on his third movie. It was called *Escape to Nowhere*. This film was set during World War II. It starred one of his sisters, Annie. The 40-minute-long movie won an award. That year, Stephen made two movies. The second one was called *Battle Squad*. It was about a German general named Rommel and his battles in Africa. Stephen used parts of a real World War II film. Then, he shot other parts that took place inside a plane on the ground. By cutting the two kinds of film together, Stephen made it look like the plane was really flying. People were amazed that a 15-year-old boy could do something so hard. But, Stephen just seemed to understand how to make a movie work. He would need this talent when he made his next film.

Make a prediction.

What do you think the author will write about next? Circle your answer.

Stephen's next movie   Stephen's mother   Stephen as a young child

Answer the following questions based on what you read on page 31. Then, finish reading the story at the bottom of the page.

1. Read the following sentence from the story and answer the question.

   By cutting the two kinds of film together, Stephen made it look like the plane was really flying.

   What does *cutting* mean in this sentence?
   a. removing
   b. taking apart
   c. combining
   d. slicing

2. Why did Stephen make his first film? Write your answer in a complete sentence.

   _____

   _____

3. Why does the author say that Stephen started a tree-selling business?
   a. He wanted to raise money to help his parents.
   b. He loved trees.
   c. He wanted to buy a present for Annie.
   d. He wanted to buy film and supplies.

4. What was the title of Stephen's fourth film?
   a. *The Last Gun*
   b. *Battle Squad*
   c. *Escape to Nowhere*

When he was 18 years old, Stephen created another movie. This one was called *Firelight*. It marked a big step for the young filmmaker. The film was a *full-length movie*. That meant it was about two hours long. Stephen borrowed $400 from his father to make *Firelight*. Stephen's sister Annie wrote the script. His sister Nancy acted in the movie.

Firelight is about UFOs that come to Earth. Later in his life, Stephen made a famous movie about friendly beings from outer space. It was called *E.T.* But, *Firelight* was scary. When *Firelight* was complete, Stephen's father rented a theater. Stephen sold tickets. He made $100 more than he spent making the movie. That same year, he started film school. So, before he had even gone to school to learn how to make movies, Stephen Spielberg was putting his stories on the big screen.

Next Page →

Movie History

Answer the questions below.

5. What is a *full-length movie*?
   a. one that is about one hour long
   b. one that has real actors
   c. one that is only about three minutes long
   d. one that is about two hours long

6. Read the following sentence from the story and answer the question.

   The movie he made next, *The Last Gun*, was a western.

   What is a *western*?
   a. a movie about life in space
   b. a movie about cowboys
   c. a movie about famous people
   d. a movie about UFOs

7. Which of the following is another word for *movie*?
   a. film
   b. cutting
   c. novel
   d. sound track

8. What is a *script*?
   a. drawings that show what the filmmaker should shoot
   b. the lines that the actors say and information about the sets
   c. a novel that the filmmaker uses to make a movie
   d. a fancy kind of writing

9. Which of the following is an opinion?
   a. Stephen found an old movie camera in his garage.
   b. Stephen's sisters helped him when he was making his first movies.
   c. Stephen's childhood was the best time for him to learn how to make movies.
   d. Stephen went to college to learn how to make movies.

10. List three adjectives or phrases that describe Stephen Spielberg.

    a. _____
    _____

    b. _____
    _____

    c. _____
    _____

Out on the Ice

The crowd was hushed as the girl skated onto the ice. Even though they had seen many skaters, this one was different. Her skating was powerful. She moved with the music. She glided with feeling. Nobody who watched was surprised when **Kristi Yamaguchi** won two awards that day. She was 16 years old at the time.

The next year, at the World Junior Championships, Kristi shone again. She skated very well. She won the gold medal! That could have been the high point of the young athlete's life. Kristi knew she could do more. She kept pushing herself. In the next four years, she won 14 first-place medals at different events. Then, she took her biggest leap: the 1992 Winter Olympics.

It had been 16 years since a female figure skater from the United States had won a gold medal. But, Kristi was ready to try. After all, she had been trying all of her life. When she was born, nobody would have guessed that she would even be able to enjoy sports.

Kristi was born with clubbed feet. She had to have casts on her legs. Later, she wore special shoes. She had trouble walking. The casts had made her legs weak. Her mother thought that Kristi should take dance classes to make her legs stronger. But, when Kristi was four years old, she watched the Olympic Games on TV. She loved the skaters. She told her mother that she wanted to skate, too.

Six days a week for 10 years, Kristi got up at four o'clock in the morning. She skated for five hours every morning . . . *before* she started school for the day! After school, she went to skating lessons. Kristi said that she learned how to do her homework and eat her meals in the car.

Make a prediction.

What do you think the author will write about next?

_____

Next Page

Answer the following questions based on what you read on page 34. Then, finish reading the story at the bottom of the page.

1. Read the following sentence from the story and answer the question.

    She kept pushing herself.

    Which of the following phrases means the same thing as *pushing herself*?

    a. pulling apart
    b. working hard
    c. doing push-ups
    d. falling down

2. Why did Kristi have to have casts on her legs?

    a. She had broken legs.
    b. She had clapped feet.
    c. She had special shoes.
    d. She had clubbed feet.

3. Why did Kristi's mother want her to take dance lessons?

    a. to help make her legs strong
    b. to help make her arms strong
    c. to help her learn how to skate
    d. a. and c.

Now, after all of her hard work, Kristi was finally trying for an Olympic gold medal.

At the Olympics, it would have been easy to be nervous. Another skater on the team, Scott Hamilton, helped Kristi. He told her to be happy and have fun. If she enjoyed her skating, it would show.

So, Kristi had fun. Everybody saw how joyful she was as she skated. Her childhood of hard work paid off. Judges watch skaters for small mistakes. If a foot is in the wrong place after a jump, or a hand doesn't look good, it costs points. When asked about her Olympic skating, Kristi said that there may only be three or four times in a skater's life when she knows that everything is perfect on the ice. For her, the Olympics was one of those times. She won a gold medal for the United States. And, she proved that hard work pays off.

Next Page

Out on the Ice

Answer the questions below.

4.–7. Write T for true and F for false.

4. _____ Kristi won her Olympic gold medal in 1990.

5. _____ Kristi skated for up to three hours before going to school.

6. _____ Kristi's Olympic gold medal was the first one for an American female figure skater in 16 years.

7. _____ A skater named Scott Hamilton helped Kristi.

8. Read the following sentence from the story and answer the question.

   That could have been the high point of the young athlete's life.

   What does *the high point* mean?
   a. the best part of somebody's life
   b. the highest place in a city
   c. a mountain peak
   d. all of the above

9. How many hours of morning practice did Kristi do in ONE WEEK?
   a. 15 hours
   b. 20 hours
   c. 30 hours
   d. 35 hours

10. List three adjectives that describe Kristi Yamaguchi.

    a. _____

    b. _____

    c. _____

11. At the end of the story, the author says Kristi "proved that hard work pays off." Fill in the following sentence to tell about a time in your life when hard work helped you.

    My hard work paid off when I

    _____

    _____

    because _____

    _____

    _____

    _____ .

Frozen Delight

How do things get invented? It happens when someone wonders, "What would happen if . . . ?"

On a night in 1905, an 11-year-old boy named **Frank Epperson** had been mixing fruit drinks. He added soda powder. He wanted to make something good to drink. Frank lived in California. The weather report said it would be very cold outside that night. Frank suddenly wondered how his fruit drink would taste if it were frozen. He put the glass outside on the porch. But, he forgot to take his wooden stirring stick out of the glass.

That night was one of the coldest nights in the state's history. The next morning, Frank went outside to get his glass. The fruit drink had frozen solid. Standing in the center was the wooden stick. Frank slid the frozen treat out of the glass and held it by the stick. He tasted it. It was good! Frank shared his new snack with his friends. He called it "the Epperson Icicle." Later, he changed the name to "the Ep-sicle."

Frank didn't seem very good at naming his new treat. He also could not make and sell it. He needed money to do that, and he didn't have any. There was another problem, too. In 1905, people did not have freezers in their homes. How would people keep the Ep-sicles frozen?

Many years passed. Frank kept inventing things. Sadly, nobody wanted to make and sell Frank's products. He was turned down over and over. Finally, Frank knew he was on his own. If one of his products would be sold, he would have to make it himself. He thought about all of the things he had invented. Which one would be the cheapest to make and sell? Suddenly, Frank thought of the Ep-sicle.

? Make a prediction.

What do you think the author will write about next?

Next Page →

**Answer the following questions based on what you read on page 37.
Then, finish reading the story at the bottom of the page.**

1. Frank Epperson invented a frozen treat

   when he was _____ years old.

2. The first name that Frank gave his treat

   was _____ .

3. Frank put his glass of fruit drink on the

   _____ .

4. The year that Frank invented his treat was

   _____ .

5. Frank's treat had a wooden handle in it
   because—
   a. he had whittled a handle just for
      the treat.
   b. he had accidentally left his stirring
      stick in the glass.
   c. he had wanted to figure out a way
      to make the treat easy to eat.
   d. a. and b.

6. What question did Frank ask himself that led
   to his new invention?
   a. What would the fruit drink taste like if it
      had a wooden stick in it?
   b. What would the fruit drink taste like if it
      were cold?
   c. What would the fruit drink taste like if it
      had soda powder in it?
   d. What would the fruit drink taste like if it
      were frozen?

Frank made a machine that molded the ice-cold snacks. He also created a machine that put his name on the wooden handles. But, it was Frank's son George who came up with a good name. George called Frank "Pop." Guess what George named his father's treat?

Frank made his icy delights by himself for two years. He sold seven different flavors. Orange was the flavor that Frank liked best. It also sold the best. In 1925, a company paid Frank so that it could make his frozen treats and sell them. Finally, Frank had sold something he had invented! Since then, this cool idea by an 11-year-old boy has become big business. People eat millions of Frank's sweet "icicles" every year.

Next Page ➡

Frozen Delight

Answer the questions below.

7. Read the following sentence from the story and answer the question.

   Frank didn't seem very good at naming his new treat.

   Is this a fact or an opinion?

   _____

8. How did Frank decide that the Ep-sicle was the invention he would make and sell?

   a. It was his best invention.
   b. People were asking for more Ep-sicles.
   c. It was the most expensive invention that he could make.
   d. It was the cheapest invention that he could make.

9. When Frank first invented his frozen treat, which two problems kept him from making and selling it?

   a. He didn't have the money, and people didn't like the treat.
   b. He didn't have a good name, and people had not heard of his treat.
   c. He didn't have the money, and people did not have freezers.
   d. He didn't want to make the treats, and he didn't have a freezer.

10. What name do you think George Epperson created for his father's frozen treat?

    _____

11. Look at the chain of events below and answer the question.

    > Frank invents a new treat when he is 11 years old.

    ↓

    > Frank invents many other things, but none of them sell.

    ↓

    > Frank invents a machine to mold the treats.

    ↓

    > A company buys Frank's idea so that it can make the treats.

    Which step is missing?

    a. Frank decides to stop inventing things.
    b. Frank decides that if he wants to sell one of his inventions, he must make it himself.
    c. Frank gives the idea for the treats to his son George.
    d. Frank gives up on the Ep-sicles and makes a new kind of cereal.

Talk to the Animals

Dylan Scott Pierce was two years old when he started to draw. He loved to draw lions and dinosaurs. Lots of young children like drawing. But, Dylan's drawings were different. They were *lifelike*—they looked like real animals. When Dylan was only nine years old, he won first place in an art contest. By the time Dylan was 10, people were lining up to buy his work. Some of his paintings have sold for $20,000!

Dylan was schooled at home. This gave him time for his artwork. Even Dylan's hobby is linked to his art. He takes photos. Sometimes, he uses his photos when he plans a painting.

Dylan's detailed paintings are sold all over the world. He likes to paint in watercolor. These thin paints help him create light and shadows when he paints animals. He has also used pencils and oil paints in his work.

Most of Dylan's paintings are of animals. Dylan has one pet, a cat. But, he loves all kinds of animals. He says sometimes he can guess what they are thinking. Dylan makes many trips to zoos. Because he is well known, the people running the zoos let him get close to the animals. He watches them. He takes pictures. One time, he even went swimming with some sea animals!

Dylan had never seen wild animals in their own habitats. At least, not until 2003 when he took a very important trip.

 Make a prediction.

What do you think the story will describe next?

_____

_____

Answer the following questions based on what you read on page 40. Then, finish reading the story at the bottom of the page.

1. What does *lifelike* mean?

   a. looking still and calm
   b. looking bright and colorful
   c. looking like something else
   d. looking real or alive

2. Read the following sentence from the story and answer the question.

   By the time Dylan was 10, people were lining up to buy his work.

   What kind of phrase is *lining up to buy his work*?

   a. a metaphor
   b. a hyperbole
   c. onomatopoeia
   d. a simile

3. List three words or phrases from the story that describe Dylan's paintings.

   a. _____

   _____

   b. _____

   _____

   c. _____

   _____

Dylan and his mother planned a trip to Africa. Dylan went on *safari*. That means he traveled into wild country. He watched animals in their natural habitats and took pictures of them. The trip lasted 27 days.

On the trip, Dylan saw all kinds of animals. Baboons jumped on the roof of the place where he stayed. He watched a herd of giraffes. One night, an elephant chased them! Later, Dylan painted a beautiful picture of an elephant. It showed how proud and free this animal was in its own home. It was a painting he could not have done after only watching animals in a zoo.

Dylan liked his trip so much that he went to Africa again. The second time, he saw lions. Dylan had painted lions for years. But, this was different. One lion looked him right in the eyes! The artist stayed in Africa for more than five weeks. He now uses some of the money he makes to help the people and wild animals of Africa.

Next Page

Talk to the Animals

Answer the questions below.

4. A *safari* is a _____

   into _____ country

   to watch _____

   _____ .

5. Read the following sentence from the story and answer the question.

   These thin paints help him create light and shadows when he paints animals.

   Which kind of paint is the subject of this sentence?

   a. oil paints
   b. acrylics
   c. watercolors
   d. none of the above

6. Why does the author say that Dylan could not have painted his picture of an elephant by going to a zoo?

   a. Zoos don't have elephants.
   b. Dylan couldn't find a zoo with an elephant that he wanted to paint.
   c. An elephant in a zoo would not have looked as free and proud as the one in his painting.
   d. Until he went to Africa, he never thought about painting elephants.

7. How old was Dylan when he first started drawing?

   a. two years old
   b. nine years old
   c. 10 years old
   d. 12 years old

8. Read the following sentence from the story and answer the question.

   Dylan's detailed paintings are sold all over the world.

   What does *detailed* mean as it is used in this sentence?

   a. filled with small details
   b. using big, broad strokes
   c. very small sized
   d. none of the above

9. List three animals other than the elephant that Dylan saw during his trips to Africa.

   a. _____

   b. _____

   c. _____

A Perfect 10

In 1967, Romania was not a free country. Laws were strict. One day, a coach there went to a kindergarten. He was looking for girls who could learn *gymnastics*, a sport that features strength and balance. He saw a little girl running and jumping. Right away, he knew he wanted to train her. The girl, **Nadia Comaneci**, spent the next eight years learning her sport. She had to work very hard. She had to do what she was told.

Nadia was tiny. When she was 14 years old, she was only 4 feet, 11 inches tall. She weighed 86 pounds. What she lacked in size, she made up in bravery. Her coach saw that Nadia had no fear of jumping, balancing, or leaping from one bar to another.

Nadia worked hard. She won medals. But, her big test would be the 1976 Olympics. She was only 14 years old. She had to travel to Montreal, Canada. She would perform in front of more than 80,000 people. Nadia was not scared. Later, she said that she did not even hear the crowd. All she thought about was her sport.

When Nadia's first score was posted, the crowd went wild. She had gotten a 10. It was a perfect score. Nobody in gymnastics had received that score before. The boards could only show scores up to 9.99! Then, Nadia did it again. She went on to win seven perfect scores.

Nadia had worked hard. Her lack of fear had helped her. She would have to be brave again in her life.

Make a prediction.

What do you think the author will write about next?

_____

Conversions

4 feet 11 inches = 1.5 meters
86 pounds = 39.01 kilograms

Answer the following questions based on what you read on page 43. Then, finish reading the story at the bottom of the page.

1. The first part of the story describes all of the following EXCEPT—

    a. how Nadia started in gymnastics.
    b. which country Nadia is from.
    c. Nadia's scores in the Olympics.
    d. what Nadia did later in her life.

2. What was Romania like when Nadia was a child?

    a. It was a free country.
    b. Laws there were very strict.
    c. It was not a free country.
    d. b. and c.

3. What is the meaning of the word *gymnastics*?

    a. a sport that features running
    b. a sport that features balance and strength
    c. a sport that features skating
    d. none of the above

4. What is one adjective that describes Nadia?

    _____

Nadia won two more gold medals in the 1980 Olympics. She won nine medals all together. She was famous all over the world. But, in her own country, her fame was not a good thing.

Nadia wanted to leave Romania and live somewhere else. People were not free to leave. Nadia was watched all of the time. She could not run away. But, she was brave. She made a plan to escape.

Nadia and six other people hiked out of Romania in 1989. They climbed in the mud and rain for six hours. Nadia came to live in the United States. She did not know if she would ever see her family again.

By 1994, things were better in Romania. The strict leader was gone. Nadia went home to visit. She went back in 1996 for her wedding. She and her husband, Bart Conner, are both Olympic stars. They teach other gymnasts. Maybe Nadia tells them her thoughts about hard work. She says, "Working hard is the only difference between being good and being the best."[1]

---

[1] "Olympic Champion Nadia Comaneci," *Young Athlete*, August 1978, http://www.gymn-forum.com/Articles/Misc-Comaneci_YA.html (accessed July 2005).

Next Page

A Perfect 10

Answer the questions below.

5. Which of the following BEST summarizes the story?

   a. Nadia Comaneci is an athlete.
   b. Nadia Comaneci's bravery helped her to win at the Olympics and escape from Romania.
   c. Nadia Comaneci now lives in the United States.
   d. Nadia Comaneci received seven perfect scores in the Olympics.

6. Read the following sentence from the story and answer the question.

   Nadia was tiny.

   What is an antonym for *tiny*?

   a. little
   b. minute
   c. even
   d. huge

7. Why did Nadia have to hike out of Romania?

   a. She was not allowed to leave.
   b. Romania was not a free country.
   c. She didn't want to live there anymore.
   d. all of the above

8. Which detail in the story shows that nobody had ever received a perfect 10 in gymnastics before Nadia?

   a. The crowd was quiet.
   b. Nadia did not hear the crowds.
   c. The boards could only show scores up to 9.99.
   d. Nadia's score was not allowed.

9. When Nadia won her gold medals in the 1980 Olympics, she was—

   a. 12 years old.
   b. 14 years old.
   c. 16 years old.
   d. 18 years old.

10. The author quotes Nadia as saying, "Working hard is the only difference between being good and being the best." Do you agree? Why or why not? Write your answer in complete sentences.

    _____

    _____

    _____

    _____

    _____

    _____

STOP

Gold Rush Fever

Conrad Reed was only 12 years old when he started the first gold rush in the United States. The biggest roadblock was his own father!

Conrad's father, John Reed, fought in the War of Independence, also known as the Revolutionary War. Then, he settled in North Carolina. He bought good farming land. All he wanted was to farm his land and live in peace. Things did not go quite the way he planned.

One day in 1799, Conrad was told to go fishing. His mother wanted to cook some fish for dinner. Conrad took his bow and arrow. He planned to shoot some fish and bring them back to the farmhouse. He walked down to Little Meadow Creek. He took aim. Then, he looked harder. Under the swimming fish was a strange rock. Conrad waded into the water. The rock was the size of a brick. It was very heavy. It looked golden. Conrad forgot about the fish. He carried the rock to his father.

His father thought the rock was interesting, too. Plus, it was useful. For three years, John Reed used the 17-pound rock as a doorstop.

Conrad turned 15 years old. His father went into town to get supplies one day. He took the rock with him. While he was in town, John went to see a jeweler. The rock was gold—17 pounds of it! Today, it would be worth about $75,000. The jeweler said he would buy the gold from John Reed. John Reed asked to be paid $3.50!

Conrad and his brothers wanted to start digging for gold on their father's farm. But, there was a problem.

Make a prediction.

What do you think the author will write about next?

_____

Conversion

17 pounds = 7.71 kilograms

Next Page

Answer the following questions based on what you read on page 46. Then, finish reading the story at the bottom of the page.

1.–5. Write T for true and F for false.

1. _____ John Reed found a strange, yellow rock in the creek.

2. _____ Conrad Reed first found gold in 1899.

3. _____ John Reed was paid $75,000 for the gold that Conrad found.

4. _____ Conrad found the yellow rock in Little Meadow Creek.

5. _____ Conrad was 12 years old when he found gold.

6. Which phrase BEST completes the following sentence?

John Reed was a soldier in _____.

a. World War II
b. The War of Independence
c. The Revolutionary War
d. b. and c.

John Reed felt that farming was a good way to make a living. He thought he could make as much money farming as he could by mining gold. So, he made a deal. Three men became his partners. These men, Conrad, and his brothers could look for gold . . . but only in the streams around the farm. They were not allowed to dig in the fields.

Every spring, John Reed plowed his land. Conrad would see pieces of gold stuck to the plow! But, he was not allowed to touch the land.

Meanwhile, other people started to talk about Conrad's big find. They said that in North Carolina you could "dig up gold like potatoes."[1] Many people came to the state to look for gold. Fifty years before gold was found in California, Conrad had started the first gold rush in the country.

Eventually, Conrad's father did allow them to mine for gold. Over the years, they found hundreds of thousands of dollars worth of gold! After Conrad died, his brothers got into a big fight about the way the money for the gold was being divided. The case was in court for 10 years. The mine closed during that time. Later, it closed for good. Today, you can visit the land where Conrad lived. You can see the stream where Conrad Reed struck gold.

[1] Wright, Renee, "Striking Gold in North Carolina," *The Carolina Connoisseur*, 2003, http://www.carolinaconnoisseur.com/gold.htm (accessed July 2005).

Next Page

Gold Rush Fever

Answer the questions below.

7. Read the following sentence from the story and answer the question.

For three years, John Reed used the 17-pound rock as a doorstop.

What is a *doorstop*?

   a. a stopper used in a door lock
   b. a weight used to hold a door
   c. a way of stopping people from going in and out
   d. a step between two rooms

8. John Reed would not let his sons dig on his land because—

   a. he wanted to keep farming it.
   b. he was not sure they had found real gold.
   c. he thought he could make money farming just as easily as he could by mining.
   d. a. and c.

9. How did John Reed learn that Conrad's rock was gold?

   a. A jeweler told him.
   b. Conrad proved it to him.
   c. He scraped off the top and saw the gold.
   d. He found more gold in his fields.

10. Which of the following words BEST describes John Reed?

   a. curious
   b. stubborn
   c. creative
   d. gentle

11. Read the following sentence from the story and answer the question.

They said that in North Carolina you could "dig up gold like potatoes."

What kind of phrase is *dig up gold like potatoes*?

   a. a metaphor
   b. a simile
   c. an idiom
   d. none of the above

12. A *gold rush* happens when—

   a. many people come to one place, hoping to find gold.
   b. many people rush to buy gold.
   c. many people try to steal gold from each other.
   d. none of the above

13. If you found gold, what would you do with the money? Write your answer in complete sentences.

   _____

   _____

   _____

   _____

   _____

STOP

The Businessman

When **Cameron Johnson** was seven years old, his mother gave him some tomatoes from the garden. He wanted to sell them. A woman asked him how much they were. When he asked for one dollar for each tomato, she said it was too much. Cameron told her it was OK. He knew that someone else might pay a dollar. He did not change his price.

That might be a key to Cameron's success. He just knows how to sell things. When he was nine years old, he got his first computer. Did he play games on it? No. He set up his first business. He sold special cards and writing paper. Cameron made everything on his computer.

Then, he started selling his sister's stuffed animals on-line. And, he bought more stuffed animals. He sold them. He made money. Soon, he was selling 40 animals each day! Cameron made $50,000 that year. He was 12 years old.

How did Cameron learn how to do this? Part of it came from his family. His family sells cars. His great-grandfather started as a car dealer. His father runs the company today. Cameron's parents also talked to him about money. He learned how to save and keep track of his money when he was young.

There's another thing that helps Cameron. He is a very good writer. He writes well about the things that he is selling. Cameron also writes for a business newspaper in Japan. He writes speeches. But that, too, is just one part of Cameron's success.

Make a prediction.

What do you think the author will write about next?

_____

Next Page ➡

Answer the following questions based on what you read on page 49. Then, finish reading the story at the bottom of the page.

1. Read the following sentence from the story and answer the question.

   Then, he started selling his sister's stuffed animals on-line.

   Which phrase could replace *on-line*?

   a. with software
   b. over a phone line
   c. on the Internet
   d. none of the above

2. A *car dealer* is—

   a. someone who designs cars.
   b. someone who sells cars.
   c. someone who collects cars.
   d. none of the above

3. Which adjective BEST describes Cameron Johnson?

   a. smart
   b. lazy
   c. cautious
   d. careless

Cameron has good ideas. Then, he acts on them. He figured out how to set up a business on his computer. Then, he did it. He acts instead of just talking about things.

He also looks for chances to sell things. One time, his father was having trouble. It was hard to tell if a sales person could call people to try to sell cars. Before making a call, a sales person had to check a list of people they were not allowed to call. This is called the "Do Not Call" list. Cameron figured out a way to use his computer to help. Now, he sells his software to other people who sell cars.

What will Cameron do next? It's hard to say. He has many ideas. He tells other kids to learn about money. Cameron has made a lot of money. He says that you don't have to do that to be happy. Many people start small businesses. The business might stay small. That's OK, says Cameron. He wants people to know that no one is too old or too young to give business a try.

The Businessman

Answer the questions below.

4. Read the following sentences from the story and answer the question.

   Cameron made $50,000 that year. He was 12 years old.

   Why do you think the author put this information in the story?
   a. These two sentences show that Cameron was a big success when he was still young.
   b. The amount of money Cameron made in one year shows how good he was at selling.
   c. The facts show that Cameron did not make as much money as he could have made.
   d. a. and b.

5. Cameron did all of the following EXCEPT—
   a. sell cards.
   b. sell software to car dealerships.
   c. sell cars.
   d. sell tomatoes.

6. According to the story, what did Cameron do when he got his first computer?
   a. He used it to play games.
   b. He used it to do his homework.
   c. He used it to set up his first business.
   d. He used it to buy software.

7. Read the following sentence from the story and answer the question.

   Cameron figured out a way to use his computer to help.

   What is another word or phrase that means *figured out*?
   a. found
   b. multiplied
   c. added up
   d. all of the above

8. List three things that helped Cameron become a success.

   a. _____

   b. _____

   c. _____

9. If you started a business, what kind of business would it be? Why? Write your answer in complete sentences.

   _____

   _____

   _____

   _____

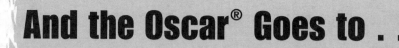

And the Oscar® Goes to . . .

Anna Paquin grew up in a home where she was "just Anna." Her brother was a dancer. He also played the cello. Her sister did gymnastics. Anna didn't get a lot of attention. In one play, her brother played Prince Charming. Anna played the part of a skunk.

Then, everything changed. Anna tried out for a part in a movie when she was nine years old. The woman who directed the movie had to pick a young girl for one of the parts. Five thousand girls auditioned for the film. Anna's sister was one of them. But, Anna got the part.

The film was called *The Piano*.[1] Anna played the part of a girl in the 1800s. Her mother could not speak. Anna and the actor who played her mother, Holly Hunter, had to look like each other. They also had to act like a mother and daughter. Anna worked with Holly every day. They made their own sign language for the movie. The movie was made in New Zealand. That is where Anna and her family lived. But, the *set* for the movie, the place where the movie was made, was an hour by plane from Anna's home. She only saw her family every two weeks. It took three months to make the movie.

When the movie came out, Anna did not see it. Her parents thought the movie was too grown up for her to see. But, people who did watch the movie thought she was amazing. Anna's part as an angry young girl with a strange mother was talked about all over the world. Then, it was time for the Academy Awards®. They are America's highest movie honors. Did Anna win an Oscar®?

Make a prediction.

What do you think the author will write about next?

_____

_____

[1] *The Piano*, directed by Jane Campion (Miramax, 1993).

Note to Teacher: This film is rated R.

Name_____ Date_____

Answer the following questions based on what you read on page 52.
Then, finish reading the story at the bottom of the page.

1. Read the following sentences from the story and answer the question.

   Anna worked with Holly every day. They made their own sign language for the movie.

   Why did the two actresses create a sign language?

   a. Anna could not speak; they needed the sign language to talk to each other.
   b. The mother in the movie could not speak; the mother and daughter used sign language to talk to each other.
   c. The movie did not have sound.
   d. The girl in the movie was deaf and needed to speak with sign language.

2. Anna Paquin—

   a. lived in New Zealand.
   b. did not see *The Piano* when it came out.
   c. once played a skunk.
   d. all of the above

3. The first part of the story tells all of the following about Anna EXCEPT—

   a. how she got her part in *The Piano*.
   b. where the movie was made.
   c. what people thought about Anna in *The Piano*.
   d. the names of her brother and sister.

Anna did win the Oscar®! She was one of the youngest actors ever to win the award. Movie offers poured in. Everybody wanted Anna to act in a movie. But, Anna took things slowly. She said that when you make a movie, your real life has to stop. She wanted to choose carefully.

When Anna was 14 years old, she made a movie called *Fly Away Home*.[2] It is the story of a girl and her father. They raise some orphan geese. Then, they help the birds migrate south for the winter for the first time. Anna had a flock of geese as her fellow actors!

As Anna grew up, she had more parts in movies. But, sometimes she still thinks she might like to be a lawyer. Whatever she chooses, few things in her life will be as exciting as her time on the big screen.

[2] *Fly Away Home*, directed by Carroll Ballard (Columbia/Sandolar, 1996).

Note to Teacher: This film is rated PG.

Next Page

And the Oscar® Goes to . . .

Answer the questions below.

4. Look at the chain of events below and answer the question.

> Anna Paquin tries for her first movie part.

> ↓

> Anna gets a part in *The Piano*.

> ↓

> Anna gets many offers to make more movies.

> ↓

> Anna acts in the film *Fly Away Home*.

Which step is missing?

a. Anna goes to college.
b. Anna's sister gets a part in a movie.
c. Anna wins an Oscar®.
d. People do not like *The Piano*.

5.–8. Match each word to its antonym.

5. _____amazing   a. carelessly

6. _____youngest   b. ordinary

7. _____carefully   c. oldest

8. _____exciting   d. boring

9. What is a *movie set*?

a. a set of cameras used to make a movie
b. a place where a movie is made
c. a script for a movie
d. all of the above

10. Read the following sentence from the story and answer the question.

Movie offers poured in.

What is another way of saying this?

a. Offers for movies were made by Anna.
b. Many people offered Anna parts in their movies.
c. Movie offers were draining away.
d. A few movie offers were made.

11. In the story, it says that Anna worked on the movie for three months and saw her family once every two weeks. This meant that while she was making *The Piano*, she saw her family—

a. about three times.
b. about six times.
c. about eight times.
d. none of the above

The Diplomat

If you have studied American history, you know about John Adams. He was the second President of the United States. You may also know about his son, **John Quincy Adams**. He also became President. But, long before he ran for office, John Quincy Adams showed that he was smart and gifted.

John Quincy was born in Massachusetts in 1767. When he was a small child, a war started with Great Britain. John Quincy watched the battle of Bunker Hill with his mother. They could see the battle from their farm.

After the war started, John Quincy's father was sent to Europe by the government. He went to France with Benjamin Franklin. They needed to get help from the French to fight the war. John Quincy's mother stayed home to run the farm.

Soon, John Quincy went to France, too. He went to live with his father. He was 11 years old at the time. After a year, the father and son moved to Holland. John Quincy went to school there. It was the first time he had gone to a school. He already knew how to speak Latin, Greek, and French. In Holland, he also learned Dutch. It never took him very long to learn a language.

When John Quincy was 14 years old, a man named Frances Dana came to see his father. Mr. Dana had to go to Russia. He was planning to ask for help from Catherine the Great. She ruled Russia at the time. But, Mr. Dana did not speak Russian. He also did not know French, which was the language spoken at the Russian court. He asked if John Quincy could go with him on his trip. John Quincy spoke perfect French.

Next Page

The Diplomat

Answer the following questions based on what you read on page 55. Then, finish reading the story on the next page.

1. The first part of the story is MOSTLY about—

   a. John Quincy Adams's early life.
   b. the life of John Quincy Adams when he was President of the United States.
   c. the life of Abigail Adams.
   d. John Quincy Adams's life in France.

2. Which of the following was one of John Quincy's talents?

   a. He could sing well.
   b. He could do hard math problems in his head.
   c. He could learn languages quickly.
   d. He could do science experiments.

3. Why did John Quincy's father go to Europe?

   a. He needed to ask for France's help in the war.
   b. He needed to travel to Russia to meet with Catherine the Great.
   c. He needed to visit Benjamin Franklin.
   d. He needed to live in Holland and learn Dutch.

4. Where was the first place that John Quincy went to school?

   a. Holland
   b. Massachusetts
   c. France
   d. Great Britain

5. Read the following sentence from the story and answer the question.

   But, long before he ran for office, John Quincy Adams showed that he was smart and gifted.

   What is a synonym for *gifted*?

   a. present
   b. silly
   c. talented
   d. witty

6. What do you think that the author will write about next? Write your answer in a complete sentence.

   _____

   _____

   _____

   _____

   _____

**Finish reading "The Diplomat" below.
Then, answer the questions on page 58.**

John Quincy left with Frances Dana on the long trip to the Russian court. He was only 14 years old, and he was already doing important work for his country. He helped Mr. Dana speak with the ruler of Russia. He went to meetings. He learned how to speak Russian. John Quincy worked for Mr. Dana for 14 months.

Then, it was time for John Quincy to leave the Russian court. He chose to travel to Holland alone. The trip was long and hard. It took six months. John Quincy made good use of the time. He planned a stop to visit the King of Sweden. During the visit, John Quincy persuaded the king to start trading with the new country that would be the United States. He was only 15 years old!

John Quincy's father thought that he was too smart to spend much time in college. He felt his son could skip part of college and study law. He wrote a long letter to the head of the law school. The letter told about John Quincy's work in Europe. It told about his talent with languages and his love of reading. John Quincy went home to America in 1785. The war with Great Britain was over.

The next year, John Quincy started college. He skipped two years and finished law school when he was just 20 years old. Later, John Quincy went back to Europe to help his country with trade agreements and treaties. Then, he became a senator, and later, the President of the United States.

Was John Quincy Adams the smartest President of the United States? Some people think so. Whether that is true or not, it is easy to see that he was an amazing kid and an amazing man. And, he lived during an amazing time in United States history.

The Diplomat

Answer the questions below.

7. Look at the chain of events below and answer the question.

> John Quincy Adams goes from Massachusetts to France.

↓

> John Quincy moves with his father to Holland.

↓

> John Quincy stops in Sweden on his way back to Holland.

↓

> John Quincy goes back to America for college.

Which step is missing?

a. John Quincy goes to Russia with Frances Dana.
b. John Quincy finishes law school.
c. John Quincy becomes a senator.
d. John Quincy becomes President of the United States.

8. Why did Frances Dana ask to take John Quincy to France with him?

a. John Quincy knew Catherine the Great.
b. John Quincy needed a break from school.
c. John Quincy could speak French, which was the official language of the Russian court.
d. John Quincy did not like living in Holland.

9. What did John Quincy do when he was 15 years old?

a. He traveled for six months on his own.
b. He met with the King of Sweden.
c. He made a trade agreement with Sweden on behalf of his country.
d. all of the above

10. Which of the following countries is NOT mentioned in the story?

a. Russia
b. Ireland
c. Holland
d. the United States

11. Read the following sentence from the story and answer the question.

Later, John Quincy went back to Europe to help his country with trade agreements and treaties.

What is a *treaty*?

a. an agreement for war between two countries
b. an agreement for peace between two countries
c. a loan of money from one country to another
d. none of the above

Be Amazing!

Maybe you have read about some amazing kids and thought, "I could never do that!" But, you can! Every kid can be amazing. Kids all over the world are doing amazing things every day.

First, you have to choose what you really want to do. Everyone has a talent. The things you like to do are clues that tell you how you can shine. People can learn to be good at all kinds of things. But, the things we love to do are often the things that we do best.

Do you love music? Would you like to play the piano or the drums? Do you like to sing? How can you learn more about music? Think about who you know. Is there someone who knows how to play the instrument you like? Maybe you do not have enough money to pay for lessons. Could you trade something instead? Maybe someone would teach you to play the piano or help you learn to sing if you raked leaves or helped in a garden. Maybe one of your teachers knows someone who could help you learn more about music, too.

Do you love to paint or draw? You can get help learning more about becoming an artist, too. Look in your local library. Ask for help finding books about learning how to draw. Go to an art show. Talk to the artists there. Take a pad of paper with you wherever you go. Draw pictures of what you see.

Maybe you love math and solving problems with numbers. How do you get better at this skill? There might be an older student who could spend some time with you. Maybe you have an older brother or sister who could teach you about what they are studying in math. And, you could help tutor younger kids. You can learn a lot from being a student and from being a teacher!

Be Amazing!

**Answer the following questions based on what you read on page 59.
Then, finish reading the story on the next page.**

1. What is the main idea of the first part of the story?

    a. Kids can be amazing if they do something they find interesting.
    b. Kids can learn more about math.
    c. Kids can learn from people and also teach people.
    d. none of the above

2. Which of the following sentences from the story is an opinion?

    a. Ask for help finding books about learning how to draw.
    b. You can learn a lot from being a student and from being a teacher!
    c. Go to an art show.
    d. How do you get better at this skill?

3. What is a *talent*?

    a. a special skill
    b. a bird's claw
    c. a piece of rope
    d. a kind of story

4. Why does the author say that every kid can be amazing?

    a. Kids do amazing things every day.
    b. All kids have special things they love to do.
    c. Kids can shine if they choose to do what they like best.
    d. all of the above

5. Which of the following is NOT mentioned as a way to learn more about art?

    a. Go to an art show.
    b. Talk to artists.
    c. Paint pictures on walls.
    d. Look for books about art in the library.

6. What does it mean to *tutor* someone?

    a. help a person with school subjects
    b. teach a whole class of students
    c. volunteer to work in the community
    d. train as a teacher

7. What do you think that the author is going to write about next? Write your answer in a complete sentence.

    _____

    _____

    _____

    _____

    _____

    _____

Next Page

**Finish reading "Be Amazing!" below.
Then, answer the questions on page 62.**

Are you interested in working with animals? Volunteer at an *animal shelter*, a place that takes care of lost and homeless dogs and cats. You can help take the animals for walks and feed them. Maybe your parents know a vet. You could talk with the vet about what it is like to be an animal doctor. Or, maybe there is a farm you could visit. You could learn more about farm life and the animals people depend on.

Do you want to make movies? Then, get started! If your family has a video camera, you can start planning to make a movie today. Some filmmakers start with a *storyboard*. This plan made of pictures shows what the camera will shoot. Ask your friends and family to play the parts. Then, go film your movie.

Maybe you are interested in helping people. There are many places where kids can make a big difference. Kids can help at community centers. They can start a drive to collect toys for a homeless shelter. They can help collect food for *food banks*, places that give food to people who need it. Kids in different places around the country help people in these ways.

You can also learn more about the kind of job you might like to have later in your life. Ask your teacher or your parents about visiting people who do that job. Sometimes, people will talk to you and show you the places where they work. You may be able to tell if you would like the job or not once you see it in "real life."

So, don't be afraid to get started. Find your gift. Look inside yourself. And, be confident. You *can* do amazing things. All you have to do is learn, try, and do!

Next Page

Be Amazing!

Answer the questions below.

8. Read the following sentence from the story and answer the question.

   You could learn more about farm life and the animals people depend on.

   Which phrase could replace *depend on* in this sentence?

   a. rely on
   b. count on
   c. hang on
   d. a. and b.

9. The story talks about all of the following things EXCEPT—

   a. what a kid could do to learn more about computers.
   b. what a kid could do to learn more about animals.
   c. what a kid could do to help people in the community.
   d. what a kid could do to learn about making films.

10. According to the story, how can you learn more about a job you might like to have someday?

    a. You could get a job like the one you want.
    b. You could ask to visit someone who does the job now.
    c. You could use the Internet to study the job.
    d. none of the above

11. What is a *food bank*?

    a. a place where people can get money for food
    b. a place where food is used like money
    c. a place that gives food to people who need it
    d. a place where you keep money

12. What is the author's purpose in writing this article?

    a. to inform
    b. to persuade
    c. to entertain
    d. a. and b.

13. What talent do you have that you would like to learn more about? How could you learn more? Write your answer in complete sentences.

    _____

    _____

    _____

    _____

    _____

    _____

Answer Key

Page 6
1. a. 2. c.
3. poor, sickly, brave
4. woman, 1960
5. c. 6. c.

Page 8
1. d. 2. c. 3. a.
4. Sputnik was a Russian satellite. It was the first satellite in space.
5. d. 6. d.
7. Answers will vary but may include: Instead of working in a coal mine, Homer grew up to work for NASA.

Page 10
1. d.
2. Answers will vary but may include: Anne and her family had to hide from the Nazis because they were Jews.
3. a. 4. F 5. T
6. F 7. T 8. T
9. d.
10. move around or make noise, the workers below might hear them

Page 12
1. c. 2. d.
3. four
4. symphony
5. school
6. split into two parts
7. b. 8. d.
9. Answers will vary.

Page 14
1. If someone is solving a calendar problem, she is given a specific date, including the year, and asked to find the day of the week for that date.
2. b. 3. F 4. T 5. T
6. F 7. T 8. b. 9. d.
10. She thinks that people need to exercise their brains.

Page 16
1. b. 2. d. 3. c.
4. c. 5. a. 6. b.
7. Answers will vary.

Page 18
1. c. 2. b. 3. a.
4. 12 years old
5. c. 6. b.
7. Answers will vary.

Page 20
1. d. 2. a. 3. e.
4. b. 5. c. 6. c.
7. a. do
   b. was not
   c. 35
8. d.
9. a. violin
   b. seven
   c. father
10. Answers will vary.

Page 22
1. Gravity
2. Christmas Day, 1642
3. learner
4. kites
5. grandmother
6. T 7. F 8. F
9. T 10. b.
11. Answers will vary.

Page 24
1. c. 2. b. 3. a.
4. d. 5. a.
6. Answers will vary.

Page 26
1. c. 2. b. 3. d. 4. d.
5. T 6. T 7. T 8. F
9. Answers will vary.

Page 28
1. a. 2. d. 3. c. 4. b.
5. 12
6. Rolfe
7. Answers will vary but may include:
   a. She carried messages from her father to Jamestown.
   b. She asked her father to give the settlers food.
   c. Her marriage helped bring peace between the tribe and the settlers.

Page 30
1. c. 2. a. 3. c.
4. Answers will vary but may include:
   a. ability to love life
   b. worked to help other children
   c. poet and hero
5. Answers will vary but may include: It would have been easy for Mattie to have given up because he knew he was going to die soon.
6. a.
7. Answers will vary.

Page 31
Stephen's next movie

Page 32
1. c.
2. Stephen made his first movie for a Boy Scouts project.
3. d.   4. b.

Page 33
5. d.   6. b.   7. a.
8. b.   9. c.
10. Answers will vary but may include:
    a. creative
    b. determined
    c. curious

Page 34
Kristi's experience at the Olympics

Page 35
1. b.   2. d.   3. a.

Page 36
4. F   5. F   6. T
7. T   8. a.   9. c.
10. Answers will vary but may include:
    a. hardworking
    b. joyful
    c. powerful
11. Answers will vary.

Page 37
Frank making Ep-sicles

Page 38
1. 11
2. the Epperson Icicle
3. porch
4. 1905
5. b.   6. d.

Page 39
7. opinion
8. d.   9. c.
10. Popsicle™
11. b.

Page 40
Dylan's trip

Page 41
1. d.   2. b.
3. Answers will vary but may include:
    a. lifelike
    b. paintings of animals
    c. watercolors

Page 42
4. trip, wild, animals in their natural habitats
5. c.   6. c.   7. a.   8. a.
9. a. baboons
    b. giraffes
    c. lions

Page 43
a time when Nadia had to be brave again

Page 44
1. d.   2. d.   3. b.
4. Answers will vary but may include: brave, talented, hardworking

Page 45
5. b.   6. d.   7. d.
8. c.   9. d.
10. Answers will vary.

Page 46
the problem with digging on the farm

Page 47
1. F   2. F   3. F
4. T   5. T   6. d.

Page 48
7. b.   8. d.   9. a.
10. b.   11. b.   12. a.
13. Answers will vary.

Page 49
Cameron's other successes

Page 50
1. c.   2. b.   3. a.

Page 51
4. d.   5. c.   6. c.   7. a.
8. Answers will vary but may include:
    a. good writer
    b. knows how to sell things
    c. has ideas and acts on them
9. Answers will vary.

Page 52
whether Anna won the Oscar®

Page 53
1. b.   2. d.   3. d.

Page 54
4. c.   5. b.   6. c.   7. a.
8. d.   9. b.   10. b.   11. b.

Page 56
1. a.   2. c.   3. a.
4. a.   5. c.
6. The author will write about John Quincy's trip to Russia.

Page 58
7. a.   8. c.   9. d.
10. b.   11. b.

Page 60
1. a.   2. b.   3. a.
4. d.   5. c.   6. a.
7. The author will write about other talents and how to learn more about them.

Page 62
8. d.   9. a.   10. b.
11. c.   12. d.
13. Answers will vary.